The Pilgrim

Al Thomas

*For Jan & David,
In memory of Bob & with deep
appreciation for your friendship.
Al Thomas*

The Pilgrim

Copyright © 2010 by Al Thomas

ISBN 978-0-557-28786-4

Scripture references are from the Revised Standard Version of the Bible, copyright © 1952 [Old Testament Section] and copyright © 1971 [New Testament Section, Second Edition] by the Division of Christian Education of the National Council of the Churches of Christ in the United States of America.

For Elaine, who shares
the pilgrimage

Contents

Introduction	7
The Road	9
The Door	30
The Garden	39
The River	44
The Valley	55
The Mountain	59
Notes	73

Introduction

The road is fresh and pleasant and green, lovely now at early dawn as the sun peeks over the hills and through the haze that yet remains, and in the near distant sky to the west a streak of burnished orange can be seen. It runs into the hills, this road, past gardens along the way, winding in such a fashion, once the mist has dissipated, as to reveal one valley after another, a meandering river uniting them, the one cultivated and lush, another untilled and overgrown, still another rich with virgin timber and yet another abundant in fissile rock.

When the rain falls upon the hills, the waters run into these valleys and feed the river that nourishes this goodly land.

As my journey in life has been commonplace, I would not speak of it now, save for the time most recent when, pausing at a vista to gaze, I heard a voice such as I never heard before, strong and gentle and kind and firm.

Why have you come, my son? Why have you come to this place?

I am a wanderer, I said.
A yearning sigh,
a rambling bye,
an alpenglow sky
to ease my bed.

You are a pilgrim, God said.
Your yearning,
a need,
a hope,
a promise,
the weaving of a thread.

The Road

I

Come; let us journey together.
I'll walk with you while you search for me.

I laughed at that and I cried at that.

I was scared; unusually, excitedly scared.

Unchaining the shackled soul, I thought, makes
wonderment possible, but responsibility necessary.

I wasn't ready for that, I knew.

I am so insignificant, Lord.
Who am I to be worthy of such attention?

To ask the wrong question
is to anticipate the wrong answer.

[I've certainly done that a time or two before.]

Let this remembrance suffice the moment.
The hyssop. I have chosen the hyssop,
a small and humble shrub,
small and humble,
to consecrate magnificent buildings
of cedar, cedars from Lebanon,
strong and mighty trees,
strong and mighty.

Where might we go, Lord?
After all,
a person can get killed going where you go.
You speak Truth where it is unwanted
lest it compromises prejudice.
You take Love where it is resented
lest it undermines self-protecting hatred.
You take Hope where it is repelled
lest it makes demands upon life.

They are your brothers and sisters.

As to people and places and things,
that is for the pilgrim road to inform.

You will, most certainly, traverse
sawdust trails
and distant vales
and cross great waters
on wind upon sails
to the promenade where people frequent,
some smiling, some reviling, some sent
to remember and repent...or forget.
Some inspired, some weary,
forspent, forspent, forspent;
some troubled, some nostalgic,
coming if convenient.

But, Lord, I am accustomed
to ribboned highways,
joined by thousands who weave a web
of interchanging lanes,
engaging in busy commerce,
with parallel lives so close yet
so unknown one to another,
traveling the tangled roads of fret,
impelled by varied demands and
frayed by conflicted dreams.

*That is not the road I called you to travel,
my son,
with its throbbing cadence and
clashing sounds and
tortured hopes.*

It is true, Lord,
I yearn for
clarity of meaning and
unhurried moments and
hushed tranquility.

I yearn for the road whose
path has way stations for the soul,
places that inspire and comfort and heal.

There are such roads.

And roads of pain, as well.

Yes, they share the path.

II

Ms. Thornton came to mind,
Alexandra by name.

[Odd, isn't it? How such happens. I had
seen her only once before, if memory serves me
correctly...maybe twice...no matter...down by the
market, I think...near Savonarola Square...a glancing
acquaintance, at most...no matter...thought she was
attractive, but we didn't speak.]

She walked her own road of pain,
laid upon by forces of oppression and harm,
and for a fleeting, flashing moment she
escaped to memories, in some way shared,
of breezy winds and flowing streams,
of tender touch and dappled dreams,
of the one and ones for whom she cared.

Then the pain returned and
she cried out to the mountain and
the God of the mountains and
she heard only echoes of her voice
till there were only echoes of echoes;
then silence, only silence,
until there were only
echoes of silence –
   forlorn,
   forsaken,
   forgotten
echoes of silence.

Then even the silence was silent, and
she was alone, till even her aloneness
was alone.

At that eternal moment,
when all hope seemed stilled forever,
out of the dawning mist,
there came a voice!

Yes, I heard her cry.
I called her softly. I called her tenderly.
My daughter, my beloved.
I inspired memories to ease her pain.
*I sent **you** to bind her wounds.*

I didn't know, Lord.
I thought I happened by.

III

We had walked the streets
in days gone by, my friend and I;
ill-lined and ill-defined retreats,
no problem for Joshua High.

Give me the winding street,
fog-shrouded, he would say.
Where's the challenge to meet –
on a straight, starlit way?

Age eighteen was Joshua High
to my sixteen when first we met;
always having to prove himself:
"I've never needed anyone yet."

He would ride the up elevator
to the down floor though he wait;
and walk up the down escalator
saying, I needn't be late.

I loved Joshua High.
He saw the world differently from any I knew.
I learned many things on fog-shrouded streets,
and some I shouldn't, 'tis true.

It was a small envelope.
I barely made out the name,
but the scribble was the same.
Joshua High.

I had not heard from him in many a year.

"Come before winter," the note entreated.
"Come before the colors fade and the petals fall.

"It is not now as were the yesterdays when
hope dawned fresh as meadow'd dew.

"I need the comfort of your presence,
the strength of your faith."

It was springtime when first we met.
The world was alive with promise, and
our paths diverged along the way
of life's crossroads.

Renew in me, O Lord, your touch
of grace that transcends words,
your love that cares beyond measure.

Winter is nigh, and I must go.

Go with my blessing, O pilgrim. Be to
Joshua as Timothy to Paul.
He needs you.

IV

There was something about Silas McGee.

Seemed to know when he was needed most,
or what words needed saying,
or when nothing needed saying
or when financial straits required his help.
[Anonymous, of course]

Some folks, yes, cross the paths of
our lives just for a while with particular gifts
by which we are enriched,

         and

some folks touch our lives
for many years, with humanity's
sweet melodies and discordant notes
intermingled, yet whose
loving concern is always clear.

Of such a tribe was Silas McGee,
full of humanity with a touch of the divine;
just a touch, mind you, admitting none.
[An iconoclast to the core, he would file a
disclaimer at heaven's door
and refuse to enter unless he won.]

Unbranded by temperament,
[Like Joshua High]
A maverick with a twinkling eye
branded by faith.

"We build community that way,"
he was quoted, "one life touching

another. We are nurtured by
memories, uplifted by affirmations,
and sustained by the sure knowledge
that the flickering flame of hope
burns more brightly."

Funny thing about Silas McGee.
He denied saying it...never said it, he
said...best of my knowledge, he
never said it...not his way of talking...
just his way of living.

Where did the words come from?
The newspaper, of all places!
Silas was voted <u>Man of the Year</u>.
Said he wasn't going to accept it.

They wrote a big, front-page article about him...
said these words described him...asked for
his picture...he said no...they said they'd use
a file picture...he said they would not.

They added a lot more words about Silas McGee.
[Don't recognize the fellow, he said.]

"We are community and to believe is to belong,"
the article continued, "the very mantra of Silas
McGee's life. It is to hold a hand to incarnate to
that person who is experiencing the soul's dark
night that 'You are loved – unconditionally.'"

Abe Mangum, my neighbor, stopped by for
coffee...said he saw Silas McGee coming
out of the newspaper office grinning.

"Canceled my subscription," Silas hollered.

"Strange thing to do, I thought," Abe muttered,
"for a man who owns the paper."

There was something about Silas McGee.

Something special! Independent! Slightly cantankerous!
A saint in training!

V

Let us go,
let us cross great waters with clear intent
to the promenade where people frequent,
where they
gather without gathering and
smile without smiling and
speak without speaking.

How are you?

Should one answer? Should one really answer?

I'm desperate to the point of death,
thank you for asking; and how are you?

The wind whispers its name, "H.H. for short,
[Hushed Hopelessness],"
and wraps it around a thousand silent voices,
muted by fears of mistrust, of rejection or the
deepest cut of all – **indifference**.
Shall one then adopt in bold defense
that very mantle as recompense
and change its name to **Nonchalance**?

Does it matter?
Does it really matter?
Does it matter that layered pretense
drives the pain for fleeting gain?

It matters! Yes, it matters.

"Is it not deception?" asked the fretting voice.

"It is survival," answered the wind, as it
whipped around the corners of untold labels
and kissed away the tears
of a thousand broken dreams
and hastened down the alleys
of a thousand frenzied schemes.

Does it matter?
Does it really matter?

"It matters," echoed the wind,
breezing across the promenade,
as it blew back the darkness
for the lingering light of God.

VI

Ms. Rainbow Jones
strolled 'cross the promenade,
[Energy in search of expression]
causing many a digression
from wireless phones
and ice cream cones.
[Cried the vendor, "Try my prawns
and the morning-fresh cod."]

"I am a seeker," said Rainbow Jones.

And, pray tell,
came a voice loud in questioning tones,
"Do you seek the knowns or the unknowns?"

"It is as it is," she replied,
"but I seek surprisingly good news!"

"'Tis of a truth," she continued, "that
Mr. Bolivar hit Mrs. Browning's car,
as she was heading to the bazaar;
and it was a mercy old Ms. Andrews escaped
in time her burning house,
and a shame Mrs. Morgenthau married such a louse;
all well reported at six on <u>Local News</u>.
Now, it was important to Mr. Bolivar, true,
to Mrs. Browning and surely Ms. Andrews,
and most certainly Mrs. Morgenthau, too.

"Yet, as one who seeks a holier grail,
I wish to glean beyond the veil.
Desiring no thrones for Rainbow Jones,
I seek only surprisingly good news,
reporting at seven on <u>Special Views</u>."

VII

We're strolling along the street at eventide.

It might not seem very important in the larger scheme
of things, but I miss the sidewalk. They don't build them
much anymore, saving money, I guess, by making
everybody walk in the street.

But streets are for cars and traffic, and not for
conversation or children playing or neighborly visit.
Streets are for destinations that take us to and fro and
sidewalks are for community that brings us together.

A sidewalk is a bridge from house to house,
a shared path that beckons one and all.
Some would say I'm just being nostalgic,
with memories refusing to yield to a new day.

I do have memories of sidewalks,
chalk-lined for hopscotch playing children,
and of the early evening stroll where
quietness of the night gave way to the caring word.

*Yes, O pilgrim, too often my people forget that what
seems to be a small thing may serve a large purpose and
fail to distinguish between what is expedient and what is
important.*

VIII

You called me to walk the second mile, Lord.
I responded with enthusiasm, but it's gotten weak.

Teach me to walk the first mile, with its compelling
discipline, that I may more faithfully walk the second.

IX

You have blessed me
in so many ways, Lord,
by your encompassing love.

So many lasting influences,
touching my life, have come
in the silence of creation.

Flowers come gradually
and silently to full bloom,
with unfolding beauty.

The first winter's snow falls
quietly, speaking of changing
seasons and glistening splendor.

Moonlight on a lake;
silvery dew in the early morning –
these are your gifts!

And yet, Lord, there is a special
gift that comes unexpectedly,
when hope is low and need is great.

Into the shattering silence there
comes a friend who speaks not
with words but caring presence.

Embodying your love, she comes
and she comes again and again
in the silence of a <u>new</u> creation.

She brings the healing of wholeness
to one who is broken and needs
above all the outstretched hand.

I am grateful, Lord, for the
influence of life upon life,
for healing with the silent touch.

X

"Thank you, Lord, for daily bread."
My friend offered a simple prayer.
We shared a simple meal.

Why bread, Lord?

So simple, yes; yet, so essential,
so defining of community.

Be gentle, O pilgrim, when you touch bread,
born of the earth yet linked to heaven's highest hopes.

It is such a common thing, this bread, so ordinary,
so commonplace; yet, you often blessed it.

Bread has no frills; yet, it has beauty in its simplicity, in
the soil giving it birth, in the sun and rain giving it
nourishment.

It draws you to the table, this bread, as love beckons
my people to gather in shared moments of caring.

Bread and caring, so yoked, so basic, so essential,
so vital as they sustain life and lives intertwined.

Remember, as I took bread in my hands and blessed it, so
I took children in my arms and blessed them.

Be gentle when you touch bread.
Be gentle when you touch life.
They are gifts of love.

XI

If in my pilgrimage I come upon a stable, Lord, what should I do?

'Tis not a place I'd usually stop to visit. Certainly, not at Christmastide! Much rather would I go to London town or Inverness or Innisfree, to Zanzibar or Kandahar or Hana by the sea.

Yet, if my path takes me to such a place on Christmas Eve, then surely it is for a purpose and that is enough.

Ah, pilgrim! There is a stable just ahead.

What a coinci…!

Go ahead and say it. The words came warmly.

I meant to say it's providential.

How strange, how alone it feels, Lord, to be in this dislocated place on this moonlit night with wintry chill the eve of Christmas, but the stable is here and I am here and it is for a reason and that is enough.

The door yields to the touch, a mingling of people, most huddling 'round a luminescent glow in the middle; some in quiet solitude along the fringe where candles flicker; still others astir, moving amidst intimations of light here and hints of darkness there. Why are they here, Lord, in this forsaken stable?

You are becoming wise, O pilgrim. Discern what you see.

'Tis not a place to be, not at Christmastide most certainly, but they are here and I am here and it is for a meaning and that is enough.

I move about...and talk...and listen...one by one.

Buffeted by winds and storms of life, Joe seeks a haven for rest and safety and hope for calmer seasons.

Troubled by doubt but longing to believe, told that the answer to faltering faith lay in a stable, Lane came forth in the haze of dawn, hoping it might be so.

The flickering candle cannot dispel the broadening shadow upon the stable floor; still, with hope Alan came at Christmastide.

Delivered from burdens that weighed him down, Hank, a man of unshackled spirit came in gratitude to this place of new birth and new beginnings.

Just now experiencing what it is to love you, Lord, a quiet radiance bespeaks Emily's presence, a love so fresh, so tender, so innocent as to be hidden almost from herself, and in her pilgrimage she seeks a stable to begin the journey.

How strange it feels to be in this dislocated place on this moonlit night with wintry chill the eve of Christmas, but they are here and you are here and I am here and it is for a blessing and that is enough.

You are growing in grace and wisdom, O pilgrim.
It is mightily so!

XII

I heard a voice saying,

Come; sing me a song of Christmas.

Sing to me your hopes.
Sing to me your fears.
Sing to me your dreams.

I am the Lord of songs.

Yes, I'll sing, O Lord of songs!

Can you hear me?
Can you hear me singing?
Can you hear bells ringing?

I sing of promises of great Christmas joy,
of the Child, of little Jesus boy.

I sing with the angels in chorus above,
the sweetest songs of dear Mary's love.

I sing of the shepherd's flock and hilly slopes,
of faltering steps and yearning hopes.

I sing of seeds no less than flowering themes,
tender blooms in my garden of dreams.

I sing of embittered brokenness made whole,
of a wondrous God healing the soul.

I sing of the victory we celebrate,
uncommon love over common hate.

Did you hear me?
Did you hear me singing?
Did you hear bells ringing,
O Lord of songs?

Yes, you sang to me a song of Christmas.

You sang to me your hopes.
You sang to me your fears.
You sang to me your dreams.

I am the Lord of songs.

XIII

With a mother's love, Mary had hoped for so much more for her first-born, but a feedbox would have to do.

Somewhere back in Nazareth, surely there remained a crib, carefully hewn in anticipation by devoted Joseph's hands, but

They were in crowded, but lonely, Bethlehem, where Mary's smile upon looking at her newborn must have become a tear as she looked at the trough.

Oh, the wonder of it, God, as that first Christmas speaks to us in this season!

Yes, it speaks one message to my children, yet differently according to need.

For those

- *who walk lonely, stabled roads to Bethlehem,*
- *who cherish a wondrous dream only to find it fading,*
- *for whom life's sweetness is too often tinged with bitterness,*
- *who cannot sleep, fearing the dream of what might have been,*
- *who see bright lights on the tree glistening through tears,*

Know that I sent my son with the promise of new beginnings.

And in some way that I do not understand, O God, you hold in your hands the stars yet were born by starlight.

XIV

Were one to ask, Lord,

would I prefer to walk in
the breaking of dawn with you,
your countenance showing the way,
        or
stroll in the quietness
of eventide with you, your
light pushing back the darkness,

I could not answer, I could not choose.

How could I choose life over life?
How could I choose joy over joy?
How could I choose love over love?

Your meditation has become a prayer.
Your questions have become your answers,
O pilgrim.

XV

I am grateful
for commonplace days
and commonplace ways,
for the routines of life
that anchor my spirit.

I am grateful
for days of wonderment,
days of inspiration,
for the surprises of life
that stir my soul.

I am grateful
above all for you, Lord;
only you bless both the
daily bowing of head and
the discoveries of a searching heart.

XVI

How is gratitude measured, Lord?
It is so personal a quality.

Is there a yardstick by which the dimensions of
gratitude can be known?

Do we recognize the grateful heart only by the fruit it
bears?

Is it as the wind comes and, though seeing it not, we feel its breeze?

Look to your heart's devotion, Is it good?
Look to your mind's dedication. Is it honorable?
Look to your soul's loyalty? Is it true?

You cannot measure the immeasurable, O pilgrim.
You will know the grateful heart by the tender touch of its presence.

XVII

I experienced the wonderment of your creation in the day just past, Lord, and remember other retreats of the heart, places where beauty of nature and acts of grace commingle.

Sometimes in the most ordinary places, I have experienced the most extraordinary gifts.

Your discernment, O pilgrim, has become a blessing.
Such places are now a shrine for you, never ordinary again.

The Door

I

"I have grown old...grown old
within these walls behind the door.
What I see", Johnny said to me,
"on either side are stranger's lore,
the one I experience, the other I am told.
Whether leaving or receiving,
it is the door of perception –
existence within, imagination without."
[Twenty years to life, he's done twenty – about.]

Top off walls with razor wire,
they aim to keep their guests a while.
That's the way Johnny described it.
Having shed no tears for many years,
he's learned to say it with a smile.

The door's not too foreboding,
just the unknown and all that.
[Not much privacy left after screening.]
A triple set of iron-grilled gates,
sliding open one at a time,
the one closing before the next opens,

suspended between past and future,
confinement and freedom.

Felt strange...very strange.

I was escorted down a lengthy hallway,
stark save for a series of photographs,
simply framed; stark themselves in black and white.
Interesting, I thought. [Appropriate, somehow]

"There's <u>Moonrise, Hernandez, New Mexico</u>," I said.

"Uh huh," she grunted, not looking in my direction.

We walked.

"There's <u>Yosemite</u>," I said.

She looked neither left nor right, nor did she speak,
grunting silently this time.
She wasn't the conversing type.
I was trying to ease my unease.
It wasn't working.

"Pictures should be a creation, not just a reminder."
That's what he said,
[The picture taker, that is]
a long time dead.
There's <u>Aspens</u>.
All those shades of gray. Interesting, I thought.
[Quite a contrast with prison regulations.]
A system of zones
for gray-scale tones.
"Perceive, then create your perception."
[Now there's a different kind of door.]
<u>Images of Freedom</u>.
They're here and not here, the images but not freedom.

"Look to the heavens. See the mountains up close
and from a distance. Listen to the running brook.
It's your heritage."

There's yet another door
beyond the visitor,
heavy and unforgiving, locked.
The door of perception?
What lies beyond
from either perspective?
Captivity or freedom?
A juxtaposition, of sorts,
making one reflective.

I thought of the images I'd seen,
hanging starkly on the wall.
Oh!... "You don't play ping-pong
in a cathedral." ...I'm sure he said that...
Quite sure! It'd be wrong.
"Something must remain that is noble, after all!"

II

Johnny said,
"I've been thinking since the time before,
the time you came, this very place;
you piqued my fancy whether the door
would lead to judgment or to grace.
It depends on whether it's opening or closing,
you said.

"For twenty years in one location,
I've walked these halls of desolation.
Is it not possible for grace to abound

within these encasing, debasing walls?
Now, I'm still unsure whether more secure,
imprisoned or free; but it seems to me,
I've found mercy and grace in this place,
walking only on this lonely, cloistered ground;
fearing still more the outside judgment halls."

"But, Johnny," I emphasized,
"no one ever sympathized
more with your plight.
You know it's right
that grace is freeing."

"You must agree," he said to me,
"that your or my state of grace
is not a matter of place;
not walls but being."

"I know," I said with great control,
"that walls cannot enslave the soul;
but as you lived within these walls
and as you wandered yonder halls,
under what condition did you find
contrition?"

"It was not," said he,
"the walls that bound me
nor the halls around me,
but the door of perception
through which walked one
fateful day, the only one who
could say, I forgive you."

"I make no condition of contrition,"
said Sue, smiling in this unsmiling place.

"For penitence, as the twilight rose,
needs nurturing soil from which it grows.
I forgive you...I forgive you.
I give you an offering of God's grace."

"At that moment I knew my sin, not before,
receiving forgiveness at discernment's door.
It was the gift of grace brought to this place,
eternal as lapping waters on the shore
and promises writ large in an ancient scroll,
that ever changed the direction of my soul:
reviling to reconciling;
chasm to a bridge;
pain to an awareness of the cost.

"Strange is the logic of God I've come to know!
Different from what I learned in schools long ago.
Unlike the echoes echoing through these halls.
Unlike the marks marking time upon these walls.
Unlike unrequited, tactless bathroom scrawls.

"Should you ask, what is it?
And reiterate, pray tell,
what is this strange,
this unusual way of God?
I would answer,
then answer again, with a question.
Who would have thought forgiveness to be justice?
Who would have thought justice and mercy to be one?"

Johnny is now free, O pilgrim, imprisoned no more.
You have ministered well to him.

III

It was on the day
of the fifth of May
[The year of our Lord Nineteen Ninety Four]
that Johnny walked out, feeling immortal.
He sheltered his eyes to watch an eagle soar,
then turned once more toward the prison door to gaze,
not having seen this side of the portal
for Seven Thousand Three Hundred Forty One Days.

IV

Rainbow Jones was waiting at the door,
waiting, just waiting, for Johnny Moore.

"As host for Channel Ten of <u>Special Views</u>,
I'm looking for surprisingly good news.
My path led me to Sue and now to you.
'I know it sounds strange,' Sue said, 'but
tell him...tell him, if you please, just the same,
that pain is never a zero-sum game.'"

"Did she...?" Johnny's voice began to fall.

"Yes," Rainbow Jones replied,
"she gave this number and said to call."

Johnny Moore gently cried.

V

The church, constructed of stone,
sits well off the boulevard,
framed by large oak trees and
a well-kept, manicured lawn.

Charles stood knocking, knocking at the door,
a broken and disillusioned man,
a flaming revolutionary of yesterday
with fires long quenched today.

Jane stood knocking, knocking at the door,
a lonely human spirit,
a wayfaring waif on the road of life
with no more strength for the journey.

Lives converge, knocking, knocking at the door,
an intermingling cacophony born
of scars of stigma and scars of scorn,
scars of suffering and scars of shame.

Some arrive at midnight,
fearing the revealing light;
others arrive at midday,
pushing back the night.

And so they come knocking, knocking at the door,
hoping against hope
that promises are true
that life is yet to be.

With memories ever so real,
belief is alloyed with question,
anticipation is tempered by dread,
and desire is moderated by pain.

Still, they come knocking, knocking at the door,
with fear submitting to hope,
cynicism yielding to trust and
doubt succumbing to faith.

Will the door be opened?
Is there someone who cares?
Will they be invited to enter?
Who will answer? Who will answer?

VI

Rainbow Jones stood knocking, knocking at the door,
till hearing unerring steps on marbled floor.

"As host for Channel Ten of Special Views,
I'm looking for surprisingly good news.

"What captured my eye as I rode by
under midday sun and nighttime sky
were the certain, uncertain steps
of the troubled and poor
who kept coming to implore,
knocking, knocking at your door,
as if claiming a shared ascendant.

"Surely, this is not by chance
[More even than circumstance]
for all these visitors who pass
along these corridors of grass
to come knocking, knocking at your door."

Came the reply:
"Unless they knew someone was home,
unless the outstretched hand said, Come,

they would not pace this boulevard.
They would not walk into our yard.
They would not quest this church of stone.
They would not cross this cared-for lawn
toward the portico and more,
to stand knocking, knocking at our door."

The Garden

I

Come,
let us go now.
Let us walk the garden path.
Perhaps, it speaks today.
You remember...
That's where it all began.

You discern me all too well, Lord.
When my devotion lags,
a loitering spirit defining the moment,
the garden calls.

As with Eden,
when I think of it,
when I think of the garden,
I think of you.

In many a garden have I walked when
in special moments I felt your Presence,
as sunset waned
and the evening air refreshed
with the fragrance of the lilac bush

and the falling dew announced
the approaching night
and the stars spoke of promises
yet to come
and I remembered simpler times,
finding wonderment in the commonplace.

The garden speaks.
It speaks of itself and beyond itself.
The garden teaches.
It teaches of the moment and eternity.
In what way does it speak to you,
O pilgrim?

II

It speaks of change.

Intermittent warmth and coolness.

Falling foliage with yet many trees
clinging stubbornly to their leaves.

Shorter days and longer nights,
nature needing its rest, its repose.

Latency for stillness, for quiescence.

Dormancy for restoring energy –
new birth, new life, new growth.

And of this learning, what is its meaning?

That change brings with it newness; do not
hold on to that which has served its purpose, and
be receptive to the quiet time that is prelude to rebirth.

III

It speaks of giving.

The wind-blown melody of rustling leaves,
upon my face a delightful breeze.

The forever sound of a flowing stream,
inviting me to pause for peace and ease.

Moistened droplets refresh,
glistening in early morning sun.

Awakened energy pierces the ground,
bursting forth with mixed crocus and daffodils.

You give us changing seasons, Lord, each with a gift,
along the winding path that beckons me.

And of this gift? What have you learned?

I need further the gift of instruction, that I have learned.
But, of the moment, this I know.
If I give for praise, that need makes my gift unworthy.
If I give grudgingly, the joy of giving escapes me.
If I give in order to receive, the reward is empty.
If I give as the rose sends forth its fragrance,
'tis an act of grace, a gift to all.

IV

It speaks of beauty.

Seasons arriving and departing as
seamless garments of many colors.

A rambling trail with heaven's loveliness
enshrined in the verdure of earth.

Promise filling the air with the thrush's sweet song
and arising from the soil with forget-me-nots.

Hummers succoring at columbine's flowers,
as earth is alive with a chorus of praise.

A moist place with cardinal flowers
and astilbes mingling with ferns, and
on the bank of the stream a holly tree
leaning across the water reaching for the sun.

An opening that frames a portrait of nature's transfigured
splendor, heath and heather far as the eyes can see.

The distant pin oak's brilliant red of fall and
dogwood's scarlet foliage in concert with
the sugar maple's fiery hues of orange and gold
inspiring me to linger a while.

Winter's sun casting shimmering rays of dancing light
upon ice crystals covering trees and brush;
innocent beauty in the garden
unmasking the blooms of life and
throwing us back upon the beginnings
of darkness and light and quiet simplicity.

And of beauty? What have you learned?

I can't live without beauty, Lord. This I have learned.
Leastwise, only the baser part of me can and
I'm unsure of that.

Find myself not seeking beauty and
I find myself not seeking you,
pilgrimage or no! It's a warning, a foretoken, it is!

The garden transient but eternal,
ever changing forever, ever new forever.
Beauty constant, beauty fading, beauty renewed.
In constancy, inspiration.
In fading, memory.
In renewal, expectation.
In all, gratitude.

The River

I

A path.
There is a path.
I have a question.
What is its purpose,
I hesitate...I struggle.
I doubt...I don't know.

I heard a voice.

There is a path, O pilgrim.
It is the questioning path.

But, Lord, I feel guilty
with such presumption.

Come; let us walk together.
Did I not give you the gift of discernment,
questioned knowledge leading to wisdom?
Do not fear the gifts entrusted to you.

What I fear is that you have a controversy with me.
You have desolated those who were foes,
making Nineveh as the desert floor.
I feel your reproach and dare not draw close,
lest the nearness betray me all the more.

Must I, dare I, risk madness to see your face,
cousin to Jeremiah, compatriot to Hamlet?
Can the heart be faithful without the mind
or the mind the heart?
Must I in kneeling bear the imprint of your wounds?
And that forever? Must I depart?

I have no case to plead before the mountains.
The hills return but echoes of my voice.
My words are silent...they are empty...
soured as the unripe persimmon...acrid ...styptic.
My mouth is constricted.
I shall speak no more.

You fear the responsibility
of gifts, O pilgrim.
Do you not know?
Have you not heard?
I judge in order to save.

Your word is ever present, Lord,
a consuming fire within my heart.
You compel me.
I can do no other, necessity driving me
beyond where my will dares to venture.
My very bones cry out and will not be stilled.

II

A place.
From a distance I heard,
as it were the noise of thunder,
a voice saying, *Come.*

I have a question.
Where is this place?

I heard a voice.

There is a place.
It is the river, the River Hope.
The river is mine.

And I went down to the river,
down by the riverside, and I trailed a
river walk till it turned sharply to the right.
There at the bend were large tupelos on both sides,
[ito opilwa]
rising with slowly tapered trunks,
crooked, furrowed to seventy feet,
with spreading branches of light brown,
[Whose outstretched fingers touch and meet,
canopied in a resting gown]
bearing thick and oblong leaves
providing shade and cover.

And from the trees I heard the voice of a bird:
As across the earth a fresh wind blows,
everything will live where the river flows.

III

Heaven and earth are one!
So says the river where its
flow from the hills takes a turn
at the bend on its way to the sea.

I like the river's bend.
[Memory and anticipation]
Looking to the west, I see the
ruffling waters coming from the hills,
continuing east to the enveloping sea.

The river is placid and serene,
flowing gently around the bend.
I like that! I need peace today,
a ripple, not a torrent.

Sometimes though,
when the rains have been heavy
and the sounds of rushing waters
call from the distance,
I come down to the river
where its pulsating energy
speaks to me of strength
and renewed determination.

There are times when I need just that word,
and you speak to me at the river's bend.

From wellspring to sea,
it travels crooked miles over
cascading falls and flat terrain
as its flow from the hills takes
a turn at the bend on its way to the sea.

I come often to this hallowed place
where life is sustained for fish and fowl,
for crickets and frogs, for rabbits and deer
and for people like me.

There is a river.
It is the River Hope.

With the evening inviting a hush,
I heard the voice of the hermit thrush:
As across the earth a fresh wind blows,
everything will live where the river flows.

IV

Shrill!
It was the voice of the thrush,
but not its song.
[There were none to sing.]
A strident, discomfiting screech,
a shrieking hoot
beyond natural pitch or reach,
scattering coveys
throughout the tupelos
and nature's boot.

Isabella (Peaches) Arbuthnot came a' tromping,
a' tromping down the path. "The river is mine," said she.

Now Isabella (Peaches) Arbuthnot was a proud woman.
She walked the Street of Main a proud woman.
She walked bitterly proud and angrily proud
and insecurely proud and selfishly proud
and haughtily proud and 'Don't get in my
way; I'll do anything I have to' proud.

Isabella (Peaches) Arbuthnot was proudly effectual,
a proud, trampling woman whose measure was gain.
Blanched and bouffantish, she wore her perpetual
scowl proudly; it hid both pleasure and pain.

Isabella (Peaches) Arbuthnot came a' tromping,
a' tromping down the path. "The river is mine," said she.

The day became as night and
all was black at the river's bend.
The sun was darkened with the moon
and did not follow the rain nor the rain the sun.
.
["Once I bought a pretty dress to wear in heavenly blue,"
said Isabella (Peaches) Arbuthnot, "...only for a few."]

No music rang from the mountains
nor echoed through the valleys
or across the hills.
The sassy mockingbird fell silent.
There were no songs to sing,
only the dying trills of the whippoorwills.

[Isabella (Peaches) Arbuthnot said, "You not remember?
By this very river I sang my praises one cold December."]

The boughs of the tupelos lay broken,
shattered branches spiraling unpatterned twills.
Lying prone were blooms of decay and reeds of rot.

["There once was a time I wished for posies,"
sighed Isabella (Peaches) Arbuthnot.]

Flowing waters ceased and the riverbed cracked
in its dryness. A dragging grasshopper neither struggled
nor yearned.

[Isabella (Peaches) Arbuthnot then turned,
"Fetch me an apple before you go.
I'll get hungry at the tupelo."]

There were no more deer nor turtles nor
turtledoves to drink from the thirsty ground.

V

*Do you remember, son of man? Do you remember the
waters of strife, the waters of Meribah?*

I remember!

Look to Ulai! What do you see?

I see a mighty ram defeated by a he-goat.

Look to Chebar! What do you see?

I see stormy winds and a saffired throne.

Look to the throne! What do you see?

I see a place where I heard,
as it were the noise of thunder,
a voice saying, *Come*.

Son of man, what do you see?

I see what was and is.
I see deep calling to deep
and darkness yielding to light
and stars transfixing the night
and land adjoining the sea.

Do you see more, son of man?

I see a rainbow in the sky,
a promise from on high,
a thunder on Sinai.

And?

I see a good land, a stubborn people.

Is there yet more, son of man?

I see what I hear –
strong words,
pulsating words,
throbbing words,
the word of the Lord.
What good are tithes without justice,
petitions without faith, nights without
vision or cisterns without water?

And?

I see captive people and enslaved hearts
yearning to be free.

VI

What is your testimony, son of man?

This is my testimony.
I see what was and is and will be.
The one who rules will be
the one who serves, bearing the
unbearable burdens of his people.

The old will dream anew and
the young will see visions and
the two will walk together.
Strength will be renewed for the journey,
and hope will soar as with wings of eagles.

What song will they sing, son of man?

They will sing a new song of good news
and great gladness.

In the distance I heard the voice of a bird:
As across the earth a fresh wind blows,
everything will live where the river flows.

VII

O pilgrim!
Heed my voice.
I have a controversy with you.

Yours is a word,
a mighty word, of judgment, Lord.

Yes, mine is a word of judgment,
and the mountains roar with its truth.

And tremor with its consequences, Lord.

Have you returned to the river, O pilgrim?
Have you sat by the tupelo?

I have not! Your judgment was swift,
and the sun was darkened with the moon
and the singing ceased, echoes

only of the dying trills of the whippoorwills,
and the waters ceased
and the bed of the river was dry.
You had spoken.
Your judgment was clear.
What more could I do?

Do you not know?
Have you not heard?
My judgment is redemptive.
I judge because I love.
Go! Go with grace, O pilgrim!
Show greatness of heart!
Go to the one who sits by the tupelo.

VIII

Where healing waters run deep,
I seek solitude; yet yield
to the Shepherd and the sheep
in the not too distant field,
where watchful eyes are gazing
with the freshness of a dream,
as lambs are safely grazing
by the flowing, healing stream.

And I look to the heavens
on many a starry night,
and I look within my heart
by the morning dawn of light;
and I see in the heavens
the stars cradled in your hand,
and I see within my heart
starlight birth in distant land.

And I think unto myself
how truly blessed I am
to sit by the healing stream
alongside the grazing lamb.
And oh what sweetness awaits
when to these waters I trod,
and any morning or night
I can see the face of God.

The Valley

I

I call upon your name, O God; still, I do not know you,
not as I desire. Tell me...tell me who you are.

I am...

*I am the one who sings the lullaby songs
to soothe the disquieted child.*

*I am the one who dances the celebrative rhythms
to affirm the joy of life.*

*I am the one who consoles the disconsolate one
to heal the breaking heart.*

*I am the one who seeks the seeking one
to strengthen the searching soul.*

*I am
now and forevermore.*

II

There are times, O God,
when words do not come,
times when the thoughts of my mind
cannot translate the strivings of my heart,
times when pain and struggle, distrust and doubt
define my season of faith; but you know my heart
and I lay it before you.

Sometimes, I come with enthusiasm, but the
emotion will not translate into words. Sometimes,
I come when troubled, but conflicting thoughts
make approaching you difficult.

Sometimes, Lord, I come out of self-discipline,
yet without motivation to pray, and
sometimes I come out of obligation,
but with a barren spirit.

You know me in these times all too well,
times when I feel distant and self-disposed;
yet, you know the struggle comes from
a believing heart. You know I love you
and that, in spite of myself, I am grateful.

It's praying time, Lord.
I have only the honesty of silence to offer.

III

The fretful sleep of night
creeps toward dawn,
bound by darkness still, and

I worry and I wonder and
I care and I feel helpless.

Then, the morning light
breaks with your promise that,
in spite of turmoil, of fear, of pain,
of tossing and tumbling,
there is assurance beyond the moment
and the word comes anew
and I arise to go where the heart has
gone a thousand times before; and
all is well with my soul.

A new day dawns,
created for possibilities that
yesterdays never knew,
a day freshly minted for muted dreams
whose silence can now be broken,
whose hopes can now be spoken,
a day untouched by flagging zeal but
touched by the hand of God.

Touch me, O God,
take my hand and hold it tight.
Walk with me. I cannot walk
alone to the promised land.

IV

Your spirit enriches in joy
and sustains in sorrow, Lord.
Oftentimes, I find wonderment
and solace in the same experience.

Sometimes to revel in joy
or reflect in sorrow, I stroll to
the music of the river,
the euphony of the hermit thrush
and the symphony of the night.

I walk along a path,
in a grove of trees,
in a dell, a dingle, a nook,
in a shady lair or along a brook,
where in solitude or in community
I hear anew that ancient voice riding the wind,
as primordial energy shakes the earth
and a new word shatters the void
and a vesperal breeze whispers my name
and life is renewed.

The Mountain

I

The shadows lengthen
and evening draws nigh.
It's been a long day and
you have walked with me.

I haven't always noticed you,
but you've always noticed me.

I've been on top of the mountain
and felt the praise of men, and
I've been in the lonesome valley
and felt the need of God.

How strange it seems, Lord, that
I needed you most on the mountain.
You were there, of course; I just didn't notice.

II

It was a wistful sound, a haunting refrain
that captivated me, coming from a small,
frame church nestled in the side of a mountain;
a man's voice the only indication anyone
was there, his voice and the plaintive chords of a guitar.
I turned aside to listen.

Come, sit with me, sweet Lord; I'm tired and need to rest.
My weary soul finds comfort at my Savior's breast.
I never meant to leave you, never meant to stray.
Was searching my heart and needing to get away.

And now, O Lord, I know, I know t'will be sublime,
coming home again, Sunday morning one more time.
Hal - le - lu - jah; Hal - le - lu - jah; Hal - le - lu - jah.

My heart was longing, longing, but knew not its need,
thinking that by leaving, it would surely be freed.
I traveled many a mile and paid a high toll
to learn it is your love that truly frees the soul.

And now, O Lord, I know, I know t'will be sublime,
coming home again, Sunday morning one more time.
Hal - le - lu - jah; Hal - le - lu - jah; Hal - le - lu - jah.

Too far I wandered, as the restless rivers flow,
trailing wailing whistles of lonesome trains that blow.
Too long, dear Lord, too long, I left the vale to roam,
but now my searching heart is calling me back home.

And now, O Lord, I know, I know t'will be sublime;
coming home again, Sunday morning one more time.
Hal - le - lu - jah; Hal - le - lu - jah; Hal - le - lu - jah.

III

On a cold day, a day cold with snow,
rounding the corner of Oak and Gregg,
I tripped over Mister Campaneau
and tumbled across his outstretched leg.

Called <u>Holy Moses</u> in derision,
he eyed me and said, "It matters none."
H. Moses Campaneau's decision
was simply to let them have their fun.

"For what does 'H' stand?" I asked,
sliding beside him to look at my knee.

He eyed me again, suspicious like.

"Henry. 'H' stands for 'Henry'. Used to
bother me some when they called me
Holy Moses, but 'tis jus' a habit. Call me
what they want. Don't bother none."

"Why the name? How did it start?"

"Prob'ly 'cause I always have my Bible with me.
Mama gave it when I left home...
marked a lot in red...wrote notes in the margin...
keep it in this waterproof bag...read it often...
like I'm still gittin' letters from her after all these years...
from Mama and the Almighty...
could call it a joint letter."

"Where do you sleep at night? The rescue mission?"

"No!" he exclaimed. "Hate nothing more than a
do-gooding rescuer. You ain't no do-gooder, are you?
[He didn't wait for an answer.] I'll be no one's
means of clearing his record 'fore the Almighty...
cleansing his conscience...trying to earn his salvation."

"What do you mean?" I asked.

Scrunching his eyes, he glanced at me slantwise.

"Never figured out how helping someone else
in order to save your own soul was anything but selfish.
I'll not be used for climbing into heaven."

"That's what they're trying to do?"

"It is mightily so! A stray quarter or dollar bill, hurrying
by, is an act of grace," he said with a contorted grin.
"A dose of mercy, though rare, is fine, but I'll take the
judgment of the Almighty any day over a duty-defined
act of kindness from one who insists on helping when it
ain't asked for...trying to salve his conscience, that's
all...I'm doing him a favor by not letting him git by with
it...being downright helpful.

"The more righteous he considers himself to be the
greater the guilt he feels for not measuring up to an even
higher standard. Then he uses self-righteousness to
resolve the guilt. It don't work...it's always there
nibbling...nibbling at the raw edges of the gut...
makes him more and more rigid and judgmental...
then he puts on a cloak of humility...becomes rigidly
humble...takes great pride in it... the most humble
man in town...brags about it...he don't give a hoot…
not really...jus' a sorry cycle."

"Sounds miserable!"

"It is mightily so! That's the way 'tis when you
try to earn your way to heaven."

"It becomes a burden, then?"

"A burden, yeah! That's it! A burden!
Why would the Almighty place
all these burdens on us?"

"What's the answer?" I asked in fascination.
"Is there no such thing as simple, unselfish,
homemade biscuits and molasses goodness?"

"The gift! The answer is to accept the gift.
The gift of grace! It is mightily so!"

"You sound like a preacher, Moses."

Arching his back, he faced me for the first time,
as one who had confirmed an anointing.

"Mama wanted me to be a preacher...
said I had the gift...said not all preachers
have it...the gift, that is."

Moses had a distant look in his eyes,
not a vacant stare, not a far away gaze,
but a journey to the backside of life where the
mountains and the valleys converged and conversed
and echoes could be heard of howling winds through
swirling eddies resisting the onrushing torrents of
overflowing streams moving inevitably toward the sea.

"How does this gift of grace change the guilt,
the self-righteousness?" I asked.

"'Cause you respond in gratitude.
You don't deserve it. You can't earn it.
'Tis a gift.

"Whatever rightness you have comes
out of being grateful, not of trying to
overcome the Almighty's reluctance."

"Why is this so difficult?"

"You earn something!
You think it's yours by right.
A gift!
You think it carries obligations.
Don't want to be obligated, especially
to the Almighty.
Want to march right up there and
'proach the gates of heaven with
all your entitlements and merit badges shiny
and up to date.

"Look here, Lord!
Aren't you right proud to see me?
As you rightly know, I'm an humble man,
willing, for starters, to sit at your <u>left</u> hand."

I had to grin. "You and God on good speaking terms?"

"It is mightily so! We quarrel, but I trust him."

"What do you do when it snows or gets really cold?"

"Oh, the winds of God keep pushing me 'long
'til I git to a safe place."

"The winds of God! What do you mean?"

"When a strong gale howls, I know the Almighty
is riding the wind and is a' calling.
I ride with him.
I hear the rumblings of storms
and know 'tis the thunder of his voice.
He sends the rain and says to it,
nourish my people.
When the needs of winter come,
he breathes on the waters,
shallow and deep, and ice is formed.
He tells the snow to fall and it comes down silently.
It falls quietly in all its delicate grandeur and grace."

Moses' voice lowered almost to a whisper as he finished.

H. Moses Campaneau sounded like an
Edenite prophet earning his living on the
side as a poet. Precarious, indeed!

I looked directly at him. "Others have
named you aptly. You are a holy man. Of love
you speak and of your need. Are you unable to receive
the gift of others?"

"There was a time, but no more."

"You are able to receive the gift of God,
but not of man?"

"That is my burden."

"You have been hurt deeply!"

He looked toward me briefly, then turned away uttering softly, seemingly just to himself: "The consequences of pain can be shared but not the pain itself."

"Yet, you seek the gift, the grace of God."

"God I trust."

"So with God you are able to commune."

"Yes!"

"How?"

"Once I saw the Almighty strolling in the morning
mist, and I asked why are you out and about, Lord?
He said he's out and about seeking those who would
not be sought. I asked do you really love that much,
Lord? He said, yes.

"I asked are you out and about looking for anyone
in particular here in the morning mist? He said, yes.
I looked around and no one else was there. Then I knew."

This time I turned away,
sitting there beside Moses, saying nothing,
with my eyes transfixed on the thousands
of Christmas lights adorning the street.

Why do they make me happy
 and sad at the same time?
More inviting than dispiriting, yes!
The season, I love. The lights, so many.

Perhaps, they promise too much! Perhaps, I expect too much!

I was startled from my reverie by Moses' canyonesque voice.

Born of experience or the gift of prescience, he observed, "The lights overwhelm you. To understand the season, you must consider one light at a time."

Astonished at his insight, I asked what he meant.

"Go by 1115 W. Elm any time during the day or night. You'll see the porch light on. The sixteen year old has been gone three weeks, and the light is a message from grieving parents to a runaway daughter...

"Farther along W. Elm, in the 1400 block next to the duplex on the left, lives a middle-aged woman, who nurtured the ideal in her garden of dreams only to find it shriveling in the dank, dark dawn of life's realities. I must dream anew, she said, and placed a candle in the window, ever illumined as a coming and going reminder of new beginnings...

"'Cross town at 824 N. Thrower Street, a dimly-burning candle symbolizes hope as the specter of illness hovers...

"Out here a ways on W. Gregg in Apt. 3-C at the Runsford apartments, there's a night-light in a newly-decorated bedroom where three day old Mary lay sleeping..."

I was dumbfounded, this man of the street suddenly as erudite as a language professor.

"How? How do you know these things? After all..."
I caught myself.

"Sometimes, when the Almighty comes a' calling
and riding the wind, he tells me these things.
Sometimes, I hear him calling, come out and about,
Moses, and walk with me in the morning mist. There
are things I need to share. Sometimes, I learn
in other ways."

Thank you, Moses. Thank you for the gift.
It is mightily so!

Tell me, O pilgrim, what have you learned from Moses?

Of learnings, Lord, there are three. Your grace abounds
beyond measure. You truly entrust your treasure to
earthen vessels. You see strength where the world sees
weakness.

IV

Send me the gifts of the wind, Lord.

Send me the gentle wind
that I may be soothed.

Send me the lively wind
that I may be refreshed.

Send me the howling wind
that I may be inspired.

Send me the winds of the Spirit
that I may be born anew.

V

I saw a light,
a shining light on a hill,
and in that light I saw a vision
and in that vision I saw the world
and I heard a voice saying, '*Come.*'
And I saw a new heaven and a new earth.

VI

I was touched by the light,
transcendent, inviting...

I reached but could not touch in return,
yet felt bathed in its warmth...

So much greater than I,
so beyond my understanding,
but not my gratitude...

VII

O, this is my Jerusalem,
this sacred mount on which I stand.
From here I've beheld grand visions
unfurled across this blessed land.

From this mount, so great and holy,
O, what wonderment I have seen.
From the hope of meek and lowly
to the beauty of pastures green.

Lord, you looked upon Lazarus and wept.
You looked over Jerusalem and wept.
For love is of a person and of a people.

You have grieved over the
killing fields of the world
across the centuries
and through the years.

Surely, you looked upon New York
and the ravaged field of Pennsylvania
and the destruction in Washington
and wept anew.

Twisted bodies amidst twisted rubble,
and we ask how the life of a person is measured.

Born a moment in time, yet akin to the ages,
each of us draws on the heritage of the past,
receiving not only its strength and glory but also
its frailty and shame; and what we do or fail to do
becomes prologue for generations yet unborn.

We receive, we give; and community is built or
destroyed that way.

How then do we measure the life of a person?

Is it in how we appropriate that which we
receive, how we expend that which we give?

Is it in how we soar beneath the wings
of your grace?

Is it as simple, yet as profoundly spiritual,
as how we love?

You have told us, Lord! Tell us anew how to love you
and how to love our neighbor as ourselves.
Lest we forget! Lest we forget!

*In your questions you will find the answer to
your questions, O pilgrim; for wisdom informs
knowledge. Know that for one to be created in my image
is for all to share that blessing. To desecrate my
image in another is to defile the same within yourself.*

VIII

We pray for our nation.
Give us strength and give us resolve.
We pray for our president.
Give him wisdom and give him grace.
We pray for the people of Iraq and Afghanistan
and other embattled lands.
Give them safety and give them hope.

We pray for our military,
who have crossed many waters
to far-away lands.
We pray for their safe return;
for those who,
remembering when roses
last bloomed by the sun-splashed terrace,
now dream anew of caring arms and pastoral farms
and simple things.

We pray for those
who'll never dream again,
whose last memory was of
desert sand and oil-stained land .

We pray for victory
out of our very human need,
out of our sense of rightness,
out of our love of country,
even as those who are our enemies
surely pray out of their own motivations.

Do you ever grow weary, Lord?

IX

I have seen love crucified by sin.
I have seen sin overcome by forgiveness.
I have seen forgiveness empowered by love.
I have seen the world die in the night of crucifixion day.
I have seen the world reborn on the morn of resurrection day.

What a vision, O pilgrim! What a vision!

Notes

PAGE.LINE*

The Road

14.10   Cf. 2 Timothy 4:21.

25.2-26.9   Inspired by the choirs of Hudson Memorial Presbyterian Church, Raleigh, NC, Christmas 2002.

The Door

30.1f   The initial setting of 'The Door' is within the medium security Federal Prison at Butner, NC.

30.7   *...the door of perception.* Symbolized in the prison by the locked door separating imprisonment and freedom.

                   See William Blake, *The Marriage of Heaven and Hell*: "If the doors of perception were cleansed, everything would appear to man as it is, infinite. For man has closed himself up, till he sees all things through narrow chinks of his cavern."

                   *Only the actual narrative lines are counted.

31.4-6   After passing through security and the sliding gates, one is escorted down a long corridor that ends at a locked door. Entry to a visitor's room is immediately on the right. A series of black and white prints by the celebrated photographer, Ansel Adams, line the right wall of the hallway.

31.8   ...*Moonrise, Hernandez, New Mexico.* A mural-sized print.

31.11   ...*Yosemite.* One of many prints of photographs taken in Yosemite National Park.

31.17   Cf. Playboy Interview: Ansel Adams, *Playboy*, Vol. 30, No. 5 [May 1983].

In contrast to ordinary photographs that were just 'visual diaries' or 'reminders of experience', Adams believed that photography should have emotion, be what Stieglitz called 'equivalents' of his feelings. "I want a picture to reflect not only the forms, but what I had seen and felt at the moment of exposure."

31.21   ...*Aspens.* A print. Excellent example of Adams' Zone System. See below.

31.24-26   Zone System – use a light meter to determine and control the range of gray-scale tones in the negatives. In such a way, the photographer creates his perception' of the subject, not just a reminder.

31.28   *Images of Freedom.* Exhibition at the Museum of Modern Art that Adams helped organize in the early 1940's.

32.1-3   In his Commencement Address, 'Give Nature Time,' at Occidental College on June 11, 1967, Adams said, "You must have certain noble areas of the world left in as close-to-primal condition as possible. You must have quietness and a certain amount of solitude. You must be able to touch the living rock, drink the pure waters, scan the great vistas, sleep under the stars and awaken to the cool dawn wind. Such experiences are the heritage of all people."

32.15-16, 18   Occidental College Commencement Address.

The Garden

39.15-40.25   I am grateful to Walter Russell Bowie whose creative imagery in his exposition of Genesis 2:8-15 [Garden of Eden] in *The Interpreter's Bible*, Vol. 1, 494f stimulated my own thoughts at this point.

41.18-22   These lines were inspired by Khalil Gibran's *The Prophet.*

The River

45.1	Cf. Hosea 4:1 – "...the Lord has a controversy..."
45.2-3	Cf. Zephaniah 2:13 – "...he will make Nineveh a desolation, a dry waste like the desert."
45.10	Cf. John Henry Newman, *Parochial and Plain Sermons, V, 296*: "Why didst thou kneel beneath His hand, but that He might leave on thee the print of His wounds?"
45.12-13	Cf. Micah 6:1-2 – "...plead your case before the mountains."
45.14-17	Cf. Jeremiah 20:7-8.
45.23-28	Cf. Jeremiah 20:9 – "...there is in my heart...a burning fire shut up in my bones, and I am weary with holding it in..."
46.3-4	Cf. Revelation 6:1.
46.15	*ito opilwa*: The Creek Indian words for 'swamp tree' [tupelo].
46.18-22	Cf. Isaiah 4:5-6 – "...over all the glory there will be a canopy...a shade by day...a refuge..."
46.25	Cf. Ezekiel 47.9 – "...everything will live where the river goes."

48.8	Cf. Walt Whitman, *When Lilacs Last in the Dooryard Bloom'd*.
	See also T.S. Eliot's *The Wasteland*.
	According to *Bird Watcher's Digest*, the hermit thrush [*Catharus guttatus*] is 'named for its retiring ways ...found in mixed woodlands all across North America. The full song of the hermit thrush is a beautiful series of flute-like notes repeated on different tones.'
48.21-22	Cf. Ezekiel 29:9b.
49.7-10	Cf. Joel 2:31 – "The sun shall be turned to darkness and the moon to blood..."
	Ezekiel 32:7 – "...make their stars dark... cover the sun with a cloud and the moon shall not give its light."
	Isaiah 13:10 – "For the stars...will not give their light; the sun will be dark at its rising..."
	Rev. 6:12 – "...the sun became black...the full moon became like blood..."
49.21	Cf. Ezekiel 31:12 – "...boughs will lie broken in all the watercourses of the land."
49.23	Cf. Isaiah 19:6 – "...reeds and rushes will rot away."

49.26-27	Cf. Isaiah 19:5b – "...the river will be parched and dry."
49.27-28	Cf. Ecclesiastes 12:5 – "...the grasshopper drags itself along."
50.4-5	Cf. Joel 1:20 – "Even the wild beasts cry to thee because the water brooks are dried up."
50.6	While used almost always in the New Testament as a title for Jesus, in the Old Testament 'son of man' was typically used as an equivalent for 'man'. God frequently addressed the prophet Ezekiel in this manner [e.g., Ezekiel 2:1], with such meaning as 'O man.' Indeed, the term is found most often in the apocalyptic writings and increasingly carries the imagery of an apocalyptic figure.
50.6-7	Cf. Ezekiel 47:19.
50.9	Cf. Daniel 8:2 – "...I was at the river Ulai."
50.10	Cf. Daniel 8:3-8.
50,11	Cf. Ezekiel 1:1 – "...I was among the exiles by the river Chebar."
50,12	Cf. Ezekiel 1:4 ['stormy winds']. Ezekiel 1:26 ['sapphired throne'].
50.14-16	Cf. Rev. 6:1.

51.19-22   These lines and several others thereafter in "The River" are drawn from *The Unfolding Story*, a narrative by the author dedicated to the Mixed Adults Class, Hudson Memorial Presbyterian Church, Raleigh, NC in August, 2009.

51.22-24   Cf. Isaiah 42:1-4.

52.1-2   Cf. Joel 2:28.

52.4-5   Cf. Isaiah 40:31.

52.7-8   Cf. Isaiah 42:10 – "Sing to the Lord a new song..."

53.14f   Cf. Psalm 23.

The Valley

55.3-13   Cf. Exodus 3:13-15.

56.1f   Cf. Romans 8:26-27.

The Mountain

68.16f   Cf. John 3:6-8.

            The same Greek word means both *wind* and *spirit*.

69.6   Cf. Rev. 21:1.

69.14-15   Cf. Daniel 9:16 – "...Jerusalem, thy holy mountain."

Rev. 21:2 – "...the holy city, new Jerusalem."